AF799919

TABLE OF CONTENTS

A NOTE FROM THE AUTHOR-

ABDUL LLOYD-BEY

T**his is a work** of nonfiction. It is my story as I remember it. All the events and experiences detailed are true and have been put down as I recall them. Some names, identities, and circumstances have been changed in order to protect the integrity and/or privacy of the various individuals involved.

Conversations in this work have been recorded as I remember them, but they have not been written to represent word-for-word documentation. I've retold them to evoke the real feeling and meaning of what was said, in keeping with the true essence of the mood and spirit of the event.

ACKNOWLEDGEMENT

All praise is due to God, the one and only creator of the universe. I thank you; I praise you and I glorify you and you alone.

Amen.

PREFACE

I just delivered a late evening auditorium talk. It was to a large group of mostly formerly incarcerated persons. It had been a long and intense workday. After work, I traveled a considerable distance to the talk's venue. I was tired. Upon arriving at the venue, I sat down with the large group of attendees and watched a two-hour documentary on prison reform. I listened intently to the documentary creators as they detailed the making of their powerful film. A parade of commentators and presenters thereafter spoke eloquently about the conditions of America's jails and prisons. They ultimately gave their opinions on America's prison reform efforts. Afterwards, I was called up to speak.

I informed the large audience about my life, struggles, and some of my more notable life achievements. I informed them that I was an attorney, Professor of Law, and author. I also informed them that I, too, was a formerly incarcerated person. I informed them that as a teenager, I was sentenced to and served nearly thirteen years in New York State prison for armed robbery offenses. I then talked about the current condition of America's criminal justice system.

I completed my talk, took numerous questions from the audience, and answered them as honestly as I could.

The event organizers began wrapping up the event. They made their final comments. It was a good event, although, by the end of the long evening, I was drained. I was ready to head home. After saying my goodbyes, I headed towards the venue's exit.

Before I could reach the exit doors, a young man hurriedly stepped in front of me, halting my determined progress. He wanted my attention. He stood there—his hair disheveled, clothes severely ill-fitting, head bowed low, and eyes darting back and forth. He would not look into my eyes.

Yet, in the sincerest of tones, he said to me, "I heard you speak about your life story this evening. Your story is amazing. You totally turned your life around."

He asked if I could give him some "real" advice on ways to overcome his past. He explained that he was also a formerly incarcerated person and was having a hard time finding success in his life. He desired to be successful. He wanted to live a fulfilling life.

I stared at him for what felt like a very long time. I heard the sincerity in his voice. I saw the sincerity on his face. I looked at him compassionately as I thought, *"Kill Yourself."* The world would be a much better place.

Why write this book? So many have asked, what is the secret to success after incarceration?

Over the years, I have conversed with many formerly incarcerated people, who sincerely believed that there were too few ways to be successful within the American society this, after gaining a criminal conviction. That is, besides "Fast money" and life on the streets. They honestly believed American society to be too unforgiving of men and women who may have made mistakes in their lives, which attracted a criminal conviction.

After a criminal conviction, many of the people with the above belief went on to sabotage their lives by earning another criminal conviction. Sometimes, they received life-term prison sentences on that second conviction. I know too many of them. Others weren't returned to prison. They went on to be brutally killed on the streets while trying to earn fast money after being released from prison. Again, they reverted to a life of crime, believing that there were few other viable, dignified avenues to be successful as an ex-con.

Too many men and women I have represented in the criminal courts, upon conversing with them, also voiced their sincere belief that, for formerly incarcerated persons, there were few viable paths to success beyond fast money. They honestly believed that their choices were limited to fast money or a menial existence. They sincerely believed this. So now, they stood with me by their sides, a judge staring down at them, and they being accused of new criminal offenses—offenses that were usually financially related.

In this book, I want to emphasize, not just to formerly incarcerated persons, but to all people, who may have had some rough patches in their lives, some hard times, some setbacks, some failings, to embrace life and not "throw it away."

In this book, I want to remind us all that all human life has been assigned tremendous value. This assignment has been done by the ultimate power, the creator of the universe, the creator of all mankind. Any message contradicting this truth, contradicting the idea of this high innate value, from anywhere or anyone, must be rejected.

Society may habitually fail to recognize the amazing potential and the tremendous worth of a fallen man or woman for whatever reason they may have fallen. Yet, as a human being, even if you are one of the fallen, you must recognize your own worth. You have tremendous potential, value, and worth. That is the truth. Let society live its lie.

In fact, it may take a miracle for society to change how it views a person who may have made some mistakes in their life. Fortunately, it does not take a miracle for a person who honestly wants to achieve real success in life to change into the amazing person the universe has created them to be. That is what this book is about.

There are different paths a man or woman can take to transform themselves into the amazing person they want to be. Understandably, the path which this book introduces may be too radical for some. Still, it is the path I have chosen. It is the path which I now share. *"Kill Yourself" — A Radical Guide to self-Development and Living a Fulfilling Life.*

“Let the Killing Begin.”

Kill Yourself—A Radical Guide to Self-development and Living a Fulfilling Life

INTRODUCTION

I stood still before the Judge. It was sentencing day. I was barely 18 years old. I was tall, black, poor, fairly intelligent, but wayward. A decent kid at heart but misguided. I had never physically harmed anyone in my life, beyond a few street fights and later some altercations while behind bars.

In my mind, I was flawed. Still, I thought I had value. I was not a total lost cause, so I believed.

As the judge stared down at me, I knew that he saw me. However, I also sensed that he didn't really see me. He saw my physical frame—a tall, black, young man, born and raised in tremendous poverty, standing before him. He also saw a young man accused and convicted of numerous armed robbery offenses and possession of a deadly weapon. That, he clearly saw.

Yet, as I looked at him, I had a faint hope that maybe this man, this "Honorable" judge, so well respected among men, would really see me. I hoped that he would see more than a poor Black kid from Brooklyn, accused and convicted of crimes. I hoped that he saw that I had some redeemable value, that I had significant value and tremendous worth. Maybe he, in all of his wisdom, would see that, as I stood before him—a first-time offender accused of criminal offenses, that I was redeemable. I hoped that he saw that I was "No Throwaway Boy."

CHAPTER ONE

EARLY LIFE STORY

As a child, I always believed that my life would end in failure; more specifically, long-term incarceration, death row. The idea of how my life would end was in my mind as far back as I could recall, seven or eight years old even. I really don't know the origin of this idea. However, with this notion in my mind, I walked through life. With this notion, I played in the playground, I laughed with my childhood friends, I went to religious services, and I attended school. While in school, I simply went through the motions. I often didn't work hard. The school work wasn't difficult. In fact, the school work was fairly easy for me when I applied myself. As a child, I was academically strong. I simply didn't fully comprehend the long-term value of school.

I was born into an impoverished family and raised in Brooklyn, New York. Although we were poor, the other children in the neighborhood and I played and laughed much and often. We may have simply accepted our poverty as normal.

I lived in a small, 3-bedroom apartment. There were ten of us who lived there. I had three brothers, four sisters, my mom, and my dad—living in that tiny space. We were a close-knit family in a close-knit community. I had many friends growing up. I was a fairly popular kid. I usually hung out with my peer group. However, I also hung around my older brothers and their friends.

There were a lot of us on that block; children of all ages. We had massive love for one another, cared for one another, and looked out for one another. Again, I really don't know how people who were so poor could still manage to have so much fun. Yet, we did.

The really good times in my neighborhood occurred when all of the peer groups, my older brothers and all of their friends, my older sisters and all of their friends, and others on our block, got together outside to hang out, joke around, and play group games.

We would organize relay races, dodge ball games, and punch-ball games (which is like stickball but using only one's fist to punch the small rubber ball). We had fun playing five-on-five basketball and flag football games.

In the wintertime, we held snowman building contests, producing some of the weirdest looking snowmen. We'd crack jokes on how bad each other's snowmen looked. We had wild snowball fights; the girls against the guys, the older kids against the younger kids, and sometimes, it was simply a free-for-all; every man, woman, and child were on their own. Anybody could get in on it. We had fun.

However, I believe that the pressure associated with poverty could be likened to a frog placed in a cool pot of water on a lit stove. When the frog first enters the water, it is cool, welcoming, and even refreshing. However, eventually, the water begins to heat up. It becomes dangerously hot. This happens while the frog doesn't even register the growing danger.

Many from that large group of childhood friends I had while growing up didn't make it out of that Brooklyn neighborhood. A number of them died tragic, violent deaths. Others became victims of the drug epidemic that swept across America during the '80s and '90s. They became severely addicted to cocaine or victims of violent drug crimes, mostly shootings.

An equally large number of them ended up in Maximum security prisons all across the state of New York. Some were arrested for money-related crimes, while others were arrested for crimes that, for which it was later discovered, that they were innocent. They were falsely arrested. Having no money to hire competent legal representation, they were subsequently wrongfully convicted and sentenced to long-term prison sentences.

CHAPTER TWO

MOVING FROM THE INNER-CITY

Although my family was extremely poor, my dad believed that a new environment, away from the gangs, drugs, and violence of the inner city, would be a better place to raise his family. So, he saved enough money to rent a small, one-family home and moved our family out of the inner city, Brooklyn, New York, to the middle-class area, Far Rockaway, Queens, New York. However, drugs, gangs, and violence were everywhere at that time; and they were surely in Queens when my family and I arrived.

I met my new best friend, Jason, when I was around thirteen years old. Jason was older than I. He was seventeen years old. He was smart and funny. He came from a solid, middle-class family. He lived in a nice house, had his own brand-new car, and was a star player on the local high school football team. Jason was my neighbor in my new middle-class neighborhood. He lived a few homes down from the home my family was now renting. Jason and others introduced me to drugs (marijuana) upon my arrival to Queens. Jason's marijuana uses later evolved, unbeknownst to me, into hardcore drug use and drug addiction; opioid pills and cocaine.

It was a mixed neighborhood. Everyone on my new block got along very well. It wasn't as close-knit as the block back in Brooklyn, but it was cool. All the kids embraced me as their new neighbor and friend. Jason and I became very close. I looked up to him as an older brother, and he treated me as his younger brother.

As Jason's love for the fast life grew, and, I believe, his love for drugs also grew, he soon began suggesting that we commit an armed robbery to get money for drugs and other material things. At first, I believed that Jason was just kidding. I soon realized that he was not. I was absolutely no angel, but armed robbery was a place I had never been. Still, all of my young life, I was steadily walking towards the persistent thoughts of eventual incarceration. Jason's suggestions to commit an armed robbery did not contradict the constant voice in my head. Eventually, I agreed to assist Jason in an armed robbery. I was sixteen years old at that time.

CHAPTER THREE

ARRIVING

AT HIGH SCHOOL

When I arrived for my freshman year at my new high school, Jason was there to meet me. He was already a senior and about to graduate. He was very popular, and he introduced me to all the popular kids. The football team was the star of the school, and Jason was a star on the school's football team.

However, there was a huge, racial divide at the school. The year before I arrived, there were full-blown race riots at the school. The year I arrived, there were many small, altercations between Black and White students and quite a few seriously violent incidences.

The underlying issues were as class-related as they were race-related. Most of the White students were middle-class. They lived in middle-class neighborhoods and lived middle-class lives. Many of the Black students, however, came from extremely impoverished parts of the neighborhood. A large group of Black students also came from the cluster of neighborhood housing developments located a few miles from the high school, (the projects). Many of the White students believed that the growing number of Black students at the historically mostly white school was culturally disruptive. A large portion of Black students believed that many among the White student body were unwelcoming, openly hostile, and blatantly racist. They also felt that the mostly White school administrators were unresponsive to the numerous complaints of racially motivated hostility and harassment of Black students.

At the high school, unlike in the neighborhood where I lived, there was much more segregation and much less race-mixing. Jason and I, however, were best friends while on our block and at school. Both Jason and I were very popular students. We were both well received by both the Black and White students at the high school. No one gave either of us trouble, Black or White.

CHAPTER FOUR

MY FRIEND JASON

I admired Jason. This was because my friend Jason, like several of my other white high school classmates, had very good lives; at least, that was what I observed from the outside. For instance, Jason had a brand-new car while still in high school. My father didn't even drive a brand-new car. My father could not afford one. Jason's parents supplied his every need and almost every want. That, too, was the case with many of my White classmates and friends.

Now, that's not to say that my White classmates and friends didn't have traditional teen issues, dating problems, acne, and sometimes even serious issues related to their parents' marital troubles. Jason had a serious acne problem that constantly annoyed him.

My Black high school friends, in contrast, often came to school with extremely serious life issues. Stories of violence, hunger, family abuse—near-death experiences of themselves, family members, or friends were not uncommon. There were occasional stories of actual death, the murder of someone they knew and loved. The Black students told these stories as they attended class or, far too often, failed to do so.

For example, my other best friend from high school, an African-American young man named Artie, was sixteen years old when we met. He lived in one of the worst public housing developments in Far Rockaway (the projects). He basically lived alone. His mother suffered from severe mental illness, and Artie had no father around. For months at a time, Artie's mother would be confined to mental hospitals or regular hospitals fighting illnesses she contracted from not properly caring for her health due to her severe mental illness, or she was simply roaming the streets for days—dazed and confused. While she was away, Artie ran the household. Artie worked a full-time job, did the laundry, food shopping, paid the bills, and took care of his mom on the rare days she did appear at the apartment. Artie often roamed the streets for hours, searching for his mom in order to bring her home before she could be injured or killed. Sometimes, Artie found her and brought her home. Other times, after long hours of searching, she would not be found.

Artie was a big, muscular young man. However, he was a gentle giant. His family was from Georgia, and he had that stereotypical country vibe about him. He was a kindhearted, easy-going person who was beloved by everyone. Artie was also a star football player for our high school football team. After school, Artie went to football practice every day and then went on to work. Even though he had a full-time job, he somehow still maintained good grades, and he graduated on time.

A lot of my other African-American friends at high school lived in the same housing project as Artie. Many of them knew Artie and his mom. A lot of them were similarly situated as Artie was while growing up. They grew up dealing with unbelievable environmental stresses. Yet, most of them did not manage it as well as Artie did. Many of them did horribly in high school. Artie had a doggedly determined mind to become successful in life. He felt that he had to be successful, and nothing was going to stop him. I believe, in his mind, his Mom, whom he loved dearly, was depending on him.

CHAPTER FIVE

A REAL EDUCATION IN RACE, CLASS AND THE AMERICAN CRIMINAL JUSTICE SYSTEM

During my senior year in high school, Jason and I were arrested and charged with multiple counts of armed robbery offenses. We were "Guilty As Charged." I knew that Jason and I would likely serve jail time because of the seriousness of the charges. I just didn't know how long. Shortly after our arrest, the District Attorney's office offered Jason a plea offer (plead guilty and avoid trial in return for leniency). The plea offer to Jason was 5 years in prison. Jason readily accepted that offer.

Jason was very pleased with the offer because, upon our arrest, Jason was immediately classified as a "Second-time-violent offender." He had previously been arrested for robbery in California, when he was eighteen years old. That robbery he committed solo. He served one year in a California jail for that crime.

I also later learned that shortly after our arrest, Jason had quietly confessed to a more recent armed robbery to the District Attorney's Office and then subsequently pled guilty. His elder brother, a well-known ex-felon, was wrongly arrested and convicted for that crime. However, it was Jason who had singlehandedly committed that armed robbery. Jason's brother, was falsely arrested and convicted for it. Still, with the judge's complete support, the District Attorney's office offered Jason what was universally seen as a "Sweetheart" deal, of 5 years flat.

Upon our arrest, I was classified as a first-time offender. I had no criminal record. Being that Jason had so many strikes against him and that we were presently facing the exact criminal charges, I absolutely assumed that any plea offer given to me would significantly be less than five years. I was very wrong. The prosecutor, with the full support of the judge and with a straight face, offered me a plea offer of 10 years flat, with the added statement, "Take it or leave it." My family and I were stunned.

Due to our limited knowledge of how much race and class mattered within the American Criminal Justice system, we made the unfortunate error of not taking those two critical factors, race and class, into consideration when assuming what my plea offer might be in comparison to Jason's. How naïve we were.

I made the silly error of believing that the worth of a man—all men—would potentially be equal in the eyes of the esteemed court. I thought, maybe, in a high school environment, race and class would be hugely relevant to some but not in the esteemed American courts.

In court, in a case this clear cut, with the distinction between Jason and I relative to age differences and distinct criminal records, I thought race and class may likely be a factor. However, I did not anticipate that it would be huge.

Maybe in society at large, where there is such a mix of people, learned and unlearned, race and class would matter to some, I believed. In court, however, I didn't think it would make such an outrageous difference.

I truly believe my father was firmer in his belief that the system would treat his son fairly.

He honestly believed that justice would be done in the courts that day. He really did not believe that the prosecutors would blatantly do what they did—exhibit clear race and class bias in their prosecution of his son. This, with the full support and cooperation of the judge. He was honestly surprised and unspeakably disappointed in the court system that he truly believed would do justice towards his son.

My father repeatedly implored the judge and the prosecutor to do better, to be just. They refused. He later told the judge and prosecutor, every time that we arrived in court thereafter that, "You are only treating my son like this (unfairly) because I am poor, and we are Black."

The judge threatened to imprison my father for voicing his clear objections to the mistreatment of his son. However, he would not be silenced.

My father, continued to send the same message to the judge and prosecutor by using my completely over-matched, fresh out of law school, court-appointed attorney as his reluctant messenger boy. My father strongly believed that because Jason was a White male, from a middle-class family, with a well-connected family-hired attorney, that the Judge and prosecutor saw redeemable value in Jason. While in me, they saw just another poor, Black kid, born in the ghetto, having no real value, nor real worth—a throwaway boy.

Additionally, my dad's respectful but stern, and repeated pleas for fairness and justice for his son, only served to enrage both the judge and the prosecutor. The open hostility that they showed my father and for me for daring to speak up against their blatant bias was very educational for me in the worst way.

It taught me that even the so-called best and brightest among men and women, those who have been elevated to high places, can often not see the true value of another human being or treat them equally.

The judge and the prosecutor continually warned that if I didn't accept the scandalous, 10-year plea offer and went to trial and lost, that the judge would definitely sentence me to more than 10-years in prison. The judge made sure to make that point absolutely clear.

Still, I contemptuously rejected the plea offer of 10 years. I decided to go to trial. I lost. I knew that I would. I was guilty and had absolutely no credible legal defense. However, my spirit wouldn't allow me to willingly go along with an openly unjust system of so-called justice. I would force the Judge and the prosecutor, even to my own peril, to do their dirty deeds, in open court, for the entire world to see. They would receive absolutely no cooperation from me. I wasn't voluntarily pleading guilty to anything nor accepting a 10-year plea offer. I was not doing it.

I was subsequently found guilty after trial and was sentenced to 12 ½ to twenty-five years in state prison. The prosecutor, shamelessly and with a straight face, pleaded with the judge to sentence me to an even longer prison term, more than 25 years. The judge, with a light wave of his frail old, wrinkled hand, dismissed the prosecutor's shameful request, with words to the effect of, "No, I believe 25-years is sufficient." The dead eyes of the judge and his slightly smirking face told me that he did not believe that I, with my baby face and slender built, would survive 12 ½ to 25 years in prison. He was apparently tickled by the notion.

I simply stared at the judge. My stare was defiant and marked with clear contempt. However, for the first time, in all the many days

I had appeared in that courtroom before that judge, he smiled.

The total dismissal of my father's pleas for justice pained me dearly. My father was a good man. He was disappointed by the criminal justice system. He really believed in the idea of fairness and justice within society, and even more within the court system. Again, he was not totally naïve to racism within American society. He was born and raised in the segregated south. I think what totally caught him off guard was the extreme, unabashedly, preferential treatment which, the combination of race and class, afforded a person in America, even within the so-called esteemed courts, where justice was supposed to be blind. He was disappointed in the Courts.

I disappointed my father too. I saw it on his face. He raised me better. Still, he never gave up on me, nor did he ever turn his back to me. My father's continued fierce support and encouragement, his battling for justice, following the difficult days after my arrest made me determined to make him proud someday. I was determined to do that. Yet, I had absolutely no clear idea exactly how.

CHAPTER SIX

ARRIVING AT STATE PRISON

Upon arriving at New York State prison, as a teenager, I began meeting and talking to many other incarcerated young men, all of who had stories eerily similar or even worse than my friend, Artie's. Most of the young men I met while in prison were high school or junior high school dropouts. Most of them came from extremely impoverished, crime-infested neighborhoods of New York City. Many lived all of their young lives in Public Housing Developments, (the projects), or were in and out of family homeless shelters or foster care, and almost all were exposed to extreme childhood violence, including murders, gang assaults, domestic violence, child abuse, child neglect, drugs, and almost always, extreme poverty. Most of them also were Black.

CHAPTER SEVEN

EDUCATION IN PRISON

My father continued his solid support and encouragement even after my arrival into New York state prison. He wrote to me often and visited me periodically. In a weird way, our relationship was strengthened after my incarceration by our desire to communicate with each other and really be understood.

Growing up, we didn't talk a lot. He used to talk to me. However, he rarely talked with me. It was not a real back-and-forth communication. However, during my father's prison visits to see me, we would often talk for hours. There was literally nothing else to do.

I went on to earn my GED while I was in state prison. I studied hard for it. I passed the exam easily with a very high score. My dad was very happy about that. My dad told me on more than one occasion, "You are going to do something very special in life." He told me that it was a vision that he had. He repeated it to me even as I was serving that 12-and-a-half-year prison sentence. My dad's strong support and constant words of encouragement helped me to slowly transform my childhood vision of death row into faith in a future brighter than long-term incarceration.

CHAPTER EIGHT

THE PRISON COLLEGE PROGRAM: "GOING TO COLLEGE"

Upon arriving at Attica state prison, one of New York's most notorious prison facilities, I learned that they were operating a small college program there. I signed up. The sad thing is that the inmate college program was removed from state prisons throughout New York State shortly after that.

The removal was a shame because the connection between drastically lowered recidivism rates and the achievement of higher education while incarcerated is a well-known fact throughout America's criminal justice community. Still, there was tremendous resistance throughout parts of society, to an inmate receiving what was essentially seen as a free education. This "Free Education" absolutely infuriated many people around New York State. It also infuriated many of the prison guards.

Many people in society as well as employees within New York State's prison facilities supported a *punishment-focused* approach to criminal justice rather than a "Rehabilitation" approach. To the punishment-minded crowd, college wasn't seen as punishment. So, although educating inmates was a well-established and clearly proven way to give a formerly incarcerated man or woman a greater chance at success in life after being released from incarceration, many people adamantly opposed it.

Many people around New York State, and the prison employees within Attica Prison, openly complained that the prison college program was also unfair because, while inmates were receiving "Free education," those who were not inmates had to pay for their children to attend college. Some of the prison guards at

Attica never hesitated to voice their open contempt for the prison's college program. Others actively worked to undermine the progress of inmates who decided to partake in it. I experienced this first hand.

Unceremoniously, I was removed from the college prison program at Attica state prison before I had hardly begun. I was in my second semester in the prison college program when, upon returning to the cell block from the prison yard activities and walking towards my cell, I stopped at another inmate's cell to retrieve an item. I believe it was a book or something for my college class, which was scheduled for that evening. This wasn't an unusual occurrence. Before inmates were locked into their cells, upon returning from the prison yard, they would often grab a book to read, a snack, or maybe some cigarettes from another inmate who was already locked into their cells. It was a common practice.

The problem was, I was not a common inmate. I was one of the inmates who happened to be enrolled in the prison's, not so popular college program. The prison guard working that evening was well-known around the prison to be a hostile figure towards inmates generally, and more particularly, inmates within the college program. So, I probably should have known better than to answer him when he told me in a hostile, menacing voice, "Get the fuck off the tier and lock in your fucking cell, now." I gave the officer a respectful but mild rebuke on how to talk to other human beings. I then proceeded to uneventfully lock into my cell. No major incident, no major drama, end of story—or so I believed.

When the time for college class arrived later that evening, all the inmates on the cellblock, who were enrolled in the college program, their cell doors opened. My cell door, however, remained closed. I was later told that I was being charged, by the prison guard, with "Disobeying a direct order" and "Causing a disturbance" within the prison. I was stunned.

The verbal exchange between that guard and I, relative to prison exchanges, happens many times a day between inmates and guards. It was not even close to being "that serious." A disciplinary writeup, "keep locked" order (inmate cannot leave their cell) was an exceptionally unusual occurrence.

Therefore, I assumed, being that it was clearly an exceptionally unusual occurrence, receiving a major writeup for a minor verbal back and forth, and that I had no history of creating disturbances in that prison, the administration would clearly see this minor incident, for what it was—minor.

I assumed that the Disciplinary Hearing Officer would hear the particulars of the disciplinary report and certainly dismiss these ridiculous charges. If anything, I thought I would receive at most a warning or maybe a few days' loss of privileges; telephone or commissary. No.

The Disciplinary Hearing Officer declared me guilty of the charges. I was thereafter sentenced to 30 days of cell confinement (borderline solitary confinement), with loss of all privileges; phone calls, commissary, etc.

Further, I was denied permission to attend college classes because the Disciplinary Officer had placed me on an administrative (30 day) cell confinement order; (Not allowed to exit the cell). I was therefore removed from the prison's college program—what a day.

It wasn't even the cell confinement, the loss of privileges, or even the removal from the college program that bothered me the most. Although, that was painful, no doubt. What bothered me the most was that I allowed myself to walk head-first, eyes-wide-open, directly into that guard's line of fire.

I knew the open hostility that this guard and many others had towards the prison's college program and towards inmates who were enrolled within it. I knew who this guard was. Still, my "Never back down" mentality produced a reflexive response to a potentially calculated action. A response, which allowed this hostile guard an easy win. I made it too easy.

The thing is, at the time, I was not aware of the well-established connection between college achievement and lower recidivism rates; (not returning to prison after release from prison). I came to learn this much later.

However, I did come to clearly understand that the focus at that facility, as well as many other prisons in New York State and around the entire country, was actually "Punishment" centered. So, names like "Rehabilitation Center" or "The Department of Corrections" were simply used to hide the fact that "Rehabilitation" was not the true focus within most of America's prisons. The true focus was on "Punishment" and "Incapacitation" (confinement), plain and simple.

I later learned that this punishment, incapacitation-centered model was also imitated by other agencies within the criminal justice system. For instance, the Department of Parole, which is the supervisory agency charged with the supervision of persons recently released from prison, has the tremendous potential to be a huge asset to formerly incarcerated persons. However, they were simply a reliable feeder of recently released persons back into the guts of the Department of Corrections. I came to learn that many of the newly released people from America's prisons were often returned to prison by the Department of Parole shortly after their release. This return was usually not for new crimes, as many folks in society might think. The return to prison is often for minor parole violations, like failing to find a job within a few months of being released from prison or for staying out a few hours past their arbitrarily assigned *curfews.*

I learned that there was an overt lack of serious focus upon re-entry management for formerly incarcerated persons, i.e., basic housing assistance, job training, job placement, and educational programs. For the thousands of men and women who return to American society as formerly incarcerated persons every year, they often need—at least initially—firm assistance with their basic needs. Generally, they don't receive it. Any assistance that they do actually receive is often too negligible for them to have a fighting chance for success after incarceration.

The disciplinary hearing and my removal from the college program was truly an eye-opening experience. It was a revelation. I realized that the prison was just that—a prison. It was not a rehabilitation center. In the final analysis, I realized that the prison didn't give two cents, whether I was successful in life or not. They frankly did not give a damn.

The experience crystallized for me that these institutions, "Departments of Corrections", prisons, whatever they called themselves, were glaringly ill-equipped and had no intention to offer me, or any other person confined there, a well-designed and meaningful program, which would guide them to become a successful man or woman after incarceration, which I know I desperately wanted to be.

They could not and would not do it. I realized that I would have to take full control of becoming a "Better me." I realized that to be successful in life, I would have to improve myself. I would have to create my own success program. I had to do it. So be it.

CHAPTER NINE

STUNNING REALIZATION

Upon the staggering realization that the "Department of Corrections" was completely ill-equipped and absolutely uncommitted to building, creating, and offering a serious rehabilitation system within the walls of their numerously controlled jails and prisons, a fire was started in me.

It began as a slow burn that would progressively grow. I could absolutely not serve 12 ½ to 25 years in prison without accumulating the talents, skills, and abilities needed to be successful upon my eventual release (from confinement). That would be a monumental disaster for me and a total disappointment to my family and loved ones. I had to find a way forward.

Unfortunately, inside the prison environment, there are so few pockets of positivity whereby one could peacefully sit, work and grow. However, if I wanted to get involved in any level of negativity, that was widely available and so very easy to find.

Beginning a journey of self-improvement and self-development within an environment so absent of the obvious tools to do so was a tremendous challenge and initial source of deep frustration, even anger. The question was, "Where do I begin?" I was not completely sure, so I decided to begin with books. So, I read.

I began devouring books of all kinds, all genres, hoping to stumble upon some direction, a way forward. Years earlier, I developed a love for reading, but during this period, it was almost obsessive. I often read eight to ten hours a day; that was fairly common.

I put particular emphasis on the true-life stories of people who had withstood great hardships in their lives and triumphed. I read the autobiographies of people who stood up to injustice and who fought for justice wherever they may have lived in the world. I read about great religious leaders and about the world's great religions. I read about great spiritual leaders and spirituality. I read books on philosophy, and I studied the views of the great philosophers. I read about world history and great civilizations, past and present. I would, over the next few years, read hundreds of books. I was learning a great deal about so many things.

My mind and view of the world began to change. I knew that this voracious reading would not reward me with the college degree that I desired. I didn't know if it would reward me with anything at all. Still, I read.

I also worked diligently on my writing. I needed to get better. I also began to think more. I would often spend hours a day in the quiet of my prison cell, just thinking. I didn't really know where any of this would lead. Actually, I didn't know if it would lead anywhere at all. However, I did know that I had to continue to work on myself. That was as much as I knew.

PHOTOS

Just turned 17 Years Old.
Within months would receive 25 years in state prison.

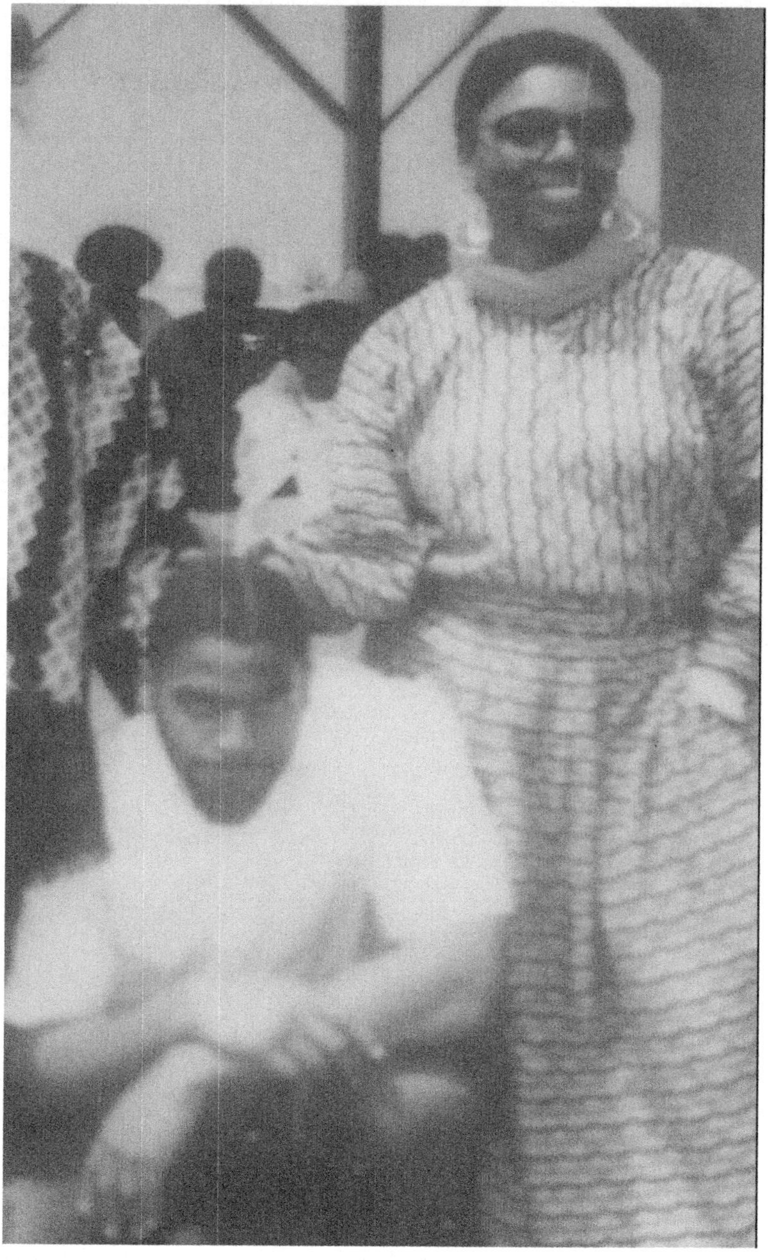

With Mom.
She always would visit and always showed love.

Dad at Graduation. It was a long journey. Good day.

Finally….home… "The Free World"

Attorney swearing in ceremony; after law school, Bar Exam, etc.

CHAPTER TEN

“KILL YOURSELF”—

YOU MUST DIE

Many years had passed since the day I was unceremoniously removed from the prison college program. I had served many years in prison at this time. I had grown a lot in that time. Still, I knew that I had much more growing to do.

I was doing a considerably larger amount of thinking at this time too. Much of the thinking now was in contemplation of what my future would be like upon release from incarceration. I realized that my teenage years were long gone. Many of my high school friends had already graduated from college. They were getting married, starting families, and some were well into their careers. This, while I was sitting in the penitentiary, serving time.

I watched many years slip by, and I still had more years to serve. I earned my GED, but I possessed no college degree. I possessed no marketable skills worthy of mention. I would be 30 years old shortly, and I didn't have a single tangible thing to show for it.

I realized that one possession, however, that I did have was a determined mind. This possession had given me the ability to build a mindset that kept me alive as I traveled into the belly of some of New York State's most dangerous prisons and jails. I did possess that. Still, I thought, "Would that mindset alone be sufficient to hand me success upon my release from incarceration?" I knew very well that a large majority of people, if not most, were not successful upon release from years of incarceration. At this point in my incarceration, I knew this to be the unfortunate and troublesome truth.

So, I knew very well that the odds of any significant degree of success after release from incarceration were statistically stacked against me.

While incarcerated, I watched as men would serve many years behind bars, be released and within one year—oftentimes even less—I would see these very same men back in the prison yard. They had been re-arrested, convicted, and returned to prison. Many times, they returned with extremely long prison sentences.

Others never returned to prison. I would later learn from other inmates, family or friends, that they had been killed while trying to get fast money, soon after being released from incarceration. This was very troubling to me. It was scary.

Upon further inquiry, I discovered that the failure to find success for most of the men and women who were going home from prison or jail was rooted in many reasons. Some were systemic. Some were not.

However, if a man or woman is convicted of a crime, even at the age of sixteen, the person is compelled to answer for that crime for their entire lives. That convicted person is forever labeled a "Felon." That designation is a stamp they must carry for life. Thus, that previously convicted person may not be able to vote, secure many types of jobs, and finding housing may be extremely difficult or nearly impossible. They may be barred from being granted certain professional licenses, and receiving certain forms of financial aid or college grants, and on and on.

This harsh, life-long exclusion from full participation in American society after serving their full debt to society, often creates a mindset of frustration, feelings of isolation, marginalization, and large-scale pessimism in these newly released men and women.

To take it a step further, newly released men and women are too often returned to their old neighborhoods after years of incarceration—poor, often homeless, or insecure in their housing situation. They arrive home with poor education, poor job skills, limited work experience, and often traumatized by their long prison experience. They could suffer from post-traumatic stress disorder, which too often goes totally undiagnosed. Even if the post-traumatic stress disorder is diagnosed, the newly released person often has no health care coverage to get or continue treatment upon their release from incarceration. I've known men to be released from incarceration and go directly back to the streets almost immediately after serving multiple-year-long lockup in solitary confinement.

Lastly, newly released persons are returning to a society that's not enthusiastically welcoming to formerly incarcerated people. This is true, particularly among the business class. So, the societal doors, traditionally used to gain access to upward mobility in American society, i.e., good jobs, securing business loans, starting a business, educational achievement, taking college courses, are often nailed shut to formerly incarcerated persons.

So, these formerly incarcerated people, some who have absolutely committed themselves to walk the straight path and others who haven't yet made that full commitment, appear in society after incarceration, often frighteningly unsure about their futures. They know the odds are statistically against them. They know society is not always welcoming to ex-offenders, skilled or unskilled, educated or uneducated. So, their mindsets upon release from incarceration, unsurprisingly, is fearful and extremely apprehensive—uncertain. It is not surprising that many of them make an unfortunate return into incarceration, usually within the first three years after being released.

I have witnessed this fearful and apprehensive "mindset" too many times. I knew about the unwelcoming society towards ex-offenders. I understood it very well.

After critically examining my mindset, I accepted the harsh reality that mine wasn't one that was ideal for success after incarceration either. I also suffered from the similar fears and apprehensions of so many other formerly incarcerated people. I was no different. Additionally, I suffered from the deviant socialization of my youth. This socialization manifested itself in actions that were often not productive, like when I could not hold my tongue when that cowardly corrections officer baited me, and I was then kicked out of the college program.

My socialization concerning how to deal with conflict resolution, disrespect (whether real or perceived), threats (real or perceived) was not the generally accepted societal norm. I was socialized to deal with conflict, disrespect, and aggression, head-on—even violently, if need be. It was a mentality absolutely ideal and acceptable on those mean Brooklyn streets and within a harsh prison environment. There it was actually admired. However, it was a mentality that would likely not hand me success in the "Free world"; life after incarceration. That's just a bit about my mindset at that time. I was concerned.

I eventually realized that to have any chance of success and living a fulfilling life after incarceration, a huge portion of my mindset and day-to-day interactions with people would have to change. Yet, I also knew that, even if I could change my mindset (which I did eventually change), the mountain of hurdles facing formerly incarcerated persons still would make success after long-term incarceration uncertain.

Ultimately, I simply concluded that if I was able to develop a mindset that was sufficient to bring me success within a harsh prison environment, then, I could likely develop a completely different mindset, one sufficient to give me a fighting chance in a completely different environment, the free world.

CHAPTER ELEVEN

THE MAN

IN THE MIRROR

I realized that I held little control over how society treats or mistreats formerly incarcerated people. Yet, I also realized that what I did have control over was my own mindset. That I could control. That was what I decided to control. Everything else, I would try not to let it depress me. "What will be, will be."

As I stood in front of the mirror, inside of my prison cell, I stared long and hard at myself. While staring intensely at my image, an interesting thing occurred. Mind you, some years earlier, I begged the creator repeatedly for His forgiveness for all the hurt, pain, disappointment, and injury I had caused to so many people.

I caused hurt and pain to my family, friends, and to society. I pled for forgiveness on so many occasions, during so many long and sleepless nights. I pled for forgiveness throughout the entirety of many days. I had hurt or disappointed so many people. Often, while alone, locked in the quiet of my prison cell, I sat regretfully, and remorsefully, shedding uncontrollable tears.

I hated so many things that I had soiled my hands with. So, as I stood in front of that mirror, I was still healing from a tremendous amount of internal pain.

Still, as I looked in the mirror, I liked the image that stared back at me. I may have even loved him. With all his scars, bruises, pain, and imperfections, I still loved him.

I loved his "Kickass" mindset. I loved his strength in the face of danger. I loved his "Never say die" attitude. I loved that he was loved, respected, and to some, even feared within the environment he now lived; one of the harshest penitentiaries in the State of New York.

Yet, as I stared at him, and he stared admirably back at me, I knew, beyond a shadow of a doubt, that I had to kill him. That was the only chance I had at surviving in my new environment—the "Free-World"; life after incarceration.

CHAPTER TWELVE

"YOU MUST DIE"

To the average person, to kill someone is not an easy thing to do. To kill someone you love is an even more difficult task. Yet, I knew it had to be done. The man in the mirror had to die.

Before I began drafting the plan to kill him, I began imagining my life after death. I envisioned myself being free from the walls of incarceration. I envisioned myself in the "Free World." I envisioned myself walking down the streets of New York City, well-dressed, nice suit, beautiful shoes, hair well-cut, happy, with a huge smile. I saw myself as a professional man. No prison garb, no prison boots. I pictured the "New me."

I envisioned myself entering a luxury car while people stared and wondered, "What does he do?" I envisioned myself entering nice restaurants with a lovely lady on my arm and being greeted by the smiling restaurant staff. I saw myself seated within the restaurant, delicious food being brought to me and my lovely date; no prison food, only the good stuff. I envisioned myself sitting at this restaurant, enjoying great food, good company, having no care in the world. I simply sat back and smiled. This was a small portion of the "New Me."

I often thought about the skills the "New Me" would need to succeed and how I would acquire them. I thought about the mindset of a "Professional" man and how I would acquire it. I also thought about the old me and how much I loved him. I then contemplated upon the many ways to kill him. I was absolutely certain that he had to die.

ACTION PLAN

PART ONE

CHAPTER THIRTEEN

STUDY YOUR PREY, STALK YOUR PREY, ANALYZE YOUR PREY, KILL YOUR PREY

If killing, dying, and death are hard for you, bail out now. The killing must be done.

Study your prey: Before you execute your plan, you must study your prey. Observe them at every opportunity. Get to know them well but be careful never to let them notice that you are watching them.

Closely observe how they walk, how they talk, observe the tone of their voice. Observe how they dress, how they wear their hair, how they eat their food, watching, even how they chew their food as they enjoy their every meal. Observe their body language, how they hold their head while walking, how they use their hands while talking, observe their facial expressions while they are still, and how they use their eyes in every occasion. Observe how they interact with others. Are they friendly? Are they shy? Are they confident? Are they reserved? Watch them. Get to know them-well.

Stalk your prey: This must be done from unseen positions. You must never be discovered. You must find a position where you can observe them, from the time they open their eyes in the morning until the time they close them to sleep. Watch what time they rise, observe if they rise early or late. Do they linger in bed upon rising, and do they pray? Do they exercise upon rising, and do they feed themselves? What do they eat, and how much of it do they consume? Are they hurried upon rising, moving frantically, or are they relaxed?

Where do they go upon rising, and what do they do? Who are their friends, and where do they live? Do they smoke, and how much of it? Where do they party, and who do they party with? Do they self-medicate, and what do they use? Do they obey the law, and when do they break it? Stalk them. This is how you really begin to know them before you kill them.

Analyze your prey,

Know your prey, Kill your prey

Finally, you must analyze all the information you have accumulated through studying your prey and then stalking your prey from positions unseen. Here, you must begin to list all that you've learned concerning the weaknesses of your prey. This part is critical and cannot be taken lightly. You cannot allow emotion, sympathy, empathy, pity, guilt, mercy, fear, or even love to cloud your judgment. You must make no excuses for your prey. You must be ice-cold and completely thorough in identifying your prey's weakness. If you fail to be thorough, your kill attempt may fail, and your prey may, unfortunately, survive your unsuccessful attempt to kill them.

Action Plan:

List the weakness:

1. ______________________________

____

2. ______________________________

____

3. ______________________________

____

4. ____

____

Etc. ______________________________________

____

Once the weaknesses are identified, you must be merciless, letting not one of them slip by. They must receive a fatal blow. They must die.

CHAPTER FOURTEEN

IMAGINING AND PLANNING LIFE AFTER-DEATH

Before you "Kill Yourself," imagine what your new life will look like. Begin to imagine your life after death. As the old you die, the new you shall emerge, but who will the new you be?

Developing, Identifying and Crafting the "New You"

In creating the "New You," you should understand very well which environment the "New You" will be entering. Then, identify the skills and the mindset that must be secured to achieve success as the "New You" within that designated environment. So, *begin securing those skills and building that mindset. Finally, identify a "New You" which will be fulfilling to you. Your life must be a life that is fulfilling to you. So, the "New You" should be a person who is pleasing to your eyes; you are the judge.*

Remember that choosing the best "New You" should not be taken lightly. It should be pondered on thoughtfully.

For instance, when thinking about the "New Me," while still incarcerated, I understood that physically, I was fairly young and very strong. However, after suffering various injuries while incarcerated, some minor and some major, I understood the human body's frailty. I understood, for instance, that if I crafted my new life to be physically labor-centered, any freak injury or simply the natural aging process could instantly push me into a *precarious financial* situation.

I knew that a number of the incarcerated men around me spoke of finding their way into the construction business, and some successfully did. Others planned future lives in the security arena, i.e., nightclubs, bars, and lounges, being that they had developed their bodies, through years of intense weight training, way beyond the size and strength of the average man. Some successfully did that too.

Although I was similarly situated, in that, since arriving in prison as a 6 foot 1, 190-pound teenager, after years of weight training, fairly clean eating, and proper sleeping, I had since grown significantly to a 6 foot 2, 250 pound, very intimidating looking, 20 plus-year-old young man. I was big and very strong, so security and/or construction work was a potential option. However, those careers didn't sit well with me as solid long-term plans.

Again, I saw the two potential pitfalls in those careers as being possible "Injury or old age." Additionally, long-term, I simply wanted my new life to be in the "Professional world." That, I believed, would be a huge part of living a fulfilling life. That was what I wanted. So, that was what I would find a way to get.

I didn't often share this vision with the folks around me. I did not want people to waste their precious time and energy trying to talk me out of what I wanted for my "New Life." I knew that out of love, not hate, people around me might attempt to encourage me to be more modest in my goals. They would not want me to suffer a major disappointment. So, I only told a few of the vision I maintained in my mind for my "New Life," the one I would achieve after long-term incarceration.

Finally, I knew that I would need to identify and develop the requisite mindset and skills I would need in my "New Life," the business or professional world.

CHAPTER FIFTHTEEN

SKILLS DEVELOPMENT

Will your life after death be in tech, business, law, sales or marketing? You must identify, list, and learn the skills you will need to succeed in that new environment.

List them

Major Skills:

1. ______________________________

____

____

2. ______________________________

____

____

3. ______________________________

____

____

Etc. ______________________________

____

____

Create the same list with “Minor Skills

You then must develop a plan to secure each one of those skills. It could be an internship, online courses, in-class courses, volunteer work in that field—whatever. Those skills must be secured.

I tried my very best to follow the above plan and acquire all the knowledge and skills I could within such a constrictive environment. For instance, a basic skill that I knew I would need was basic computer skills. I did not know hardly anything about computers.

There may have been a major plan to put "A computer on every desk and in every home," but there definitely was no plan to put a computer in every prison cell. I definitely did not have one in my cell during my many years of incarceration.

I had to find thoughtful ways to get these basic skills. I actively sought out prison work assignments where I would have as much access to prison office computers, which were sparsely placed around the various institutions I was confined in. Even if I could get a little bit of access to a computer, that would at least begin the process. I would then simply continue the learning process as a priority as soon as I was released.

Mindset Development

You must identify the key components of the mindset you must secure to be successful within your new environment.

LIST THEM

Example below:

1. Confidence
2. Assertiveness
3. Resilience
4. Fortitude
5. Patience

Structure a plan to begin developing each of those attributes. You must find a way. It could be through martial arts training, boxing classes, public speaking classes, online courses, in-class courses, one-on-one coaching, or intensive therapy. The mindset must be secured.

Always remember that this rebirth will not be a quick journey. It takes time and hard work. Your first birth was a nine-month journey. This rebirth too will take time. It will not happen overnight but begin the journey. Prepare for Life-After death.

CHAPTER SIXTEEN

"THE KILLING"- A *VISUALIZATION*

After completing the earlier described preparation to the very best of my ability, it was time. It had to be done. So, I did what I had to do. It was done.

Upon realizing that he was about to die, the man in the mirror did not panic nor make any frantic sounds. I sensed that he wouldn't. I knew him well. He had prepared for a day like this since he was a child. He always sensed that his end would likely be different from most. His eyes showed no surprise. His face showed a relaxed acceptance. He merely stared. As he took his last breathes, his eyes locked intensely with mine. My eyes flooded with tears. However, his eyes said to me, "Do not cry."

His eyes told me, "I understand." There was no hint of anger, disappointment, or sadness. "I know that you are about to go on a journey, and I cannot go along. I would only cause you trouble every step along the way," his eyes said. "I lived how I lived so that this day could be available to you someday. Today is that day. Do not judge me harshly."

"Begin your journey, and make your Father proud. Make me proud too," his eyes said. He stared at me, more intensely, as he lightly nodded his head affirmatively, his eyes saying, "Kickass man, I will always root for you. Be great."

I watched his eyes close slowly, and I cried. I cried as I have never cried before—the tears flooded up from the deepest part of my soul. I cried heavily for him because I knew him. I knew him so well. I knew the world which had created him. I knew that he lived and grew up in a world that often contemptuously looked down upon him; that disrespected his very existence.

I also knew that poverty had begun to tug at his soul. I knew that his spirit would not allow him to be bowed by anything or anyone in this world. I knew that he simply wanted to be respected as a "Man," someone who had value and worth that was equal to any other man in this world. He, therefore, would not allow anyone or anything to ever stain that desire. He believed that if standing up for that basic belief meant fighting with anyone, then so be it. I understood him. I knew him well. He was who he believed he had to be in order to simply be respected as a man.

I only hoped that he knew that, whatever "New World," I would eventually enter, that I too would never compromise my principles and be anything less than a man, ever.

I would move forward with thoughtfulness, principles, and determination. However, I would not compromise my values and my principles as a man.

After his death, there was no funeral. No notice was sent of his demise. I believe he would prefer it that way. Gently, with honor and respect, I moved him to a tranquil place. A place that was peaceful, serene, where he could rest. After saying my solemn goodbyes, I departed while promising that, "I will not let you down."

CHAPTER SEVENTEEN

MOVING FORWARD

After the killing, the thought of him stayed on my mind. However, the thought of finally leaving prison stayed at the forefront of my mind as my potential release date became nearer. I strongly believed that I was prepared. I had taken all of the requisite steps as detailed earlier. I worked intensely on myself. I was far from perfect, but I was moving forward. I was committed to doing the hard work of self-development.

Luckily, a few short years before my eventual release from incarceration, my prison classification was changed from "Maximum-security" to "Medium Security." I was shortly thereafter transferred from the maximum-security facility I had been in for many years to a medium-security prison facility located just a very short distance from New York City. I was moved closer to home. The transfer order to this facility came out of the blue. Although it was not completely unexpected. Still, it was absolutely welcomed.

Additionally, the transfer was to a facility that was in the process of phasing out their college prison program. However, upon my arrival, it had not been totally phased out yet. I immediately enrolled. The "New Me" would hold his tongue. He will not allow a hostile hater to steal this opportunity. No way.

CHAPTER EIGHTEEN

FREE!

Free! After nearly 13 years of incarceration, I took my first step into the "New World." I would continue to work on and execute my plan. I would continue to work on my self-development. I would become the person I wanted to be.

The transition from long-term incarceration into the new environment, the free-world, was not totally easy. The adjustment was often challenging. There was so much that I did not know and had to learn through hard lessons; missteps, mistakes, and setbacks.

Irrespective of any challenge I encountered, I vowed to continue to work the plan and stay committed to becoming the outstanding, engaging professional man that I desired to be.

There were times when I had no job, little money, or a low-paying job, with long hours and extremely hard work. Yet, finally, I was hired at my first, low-paying, professional, entry-level position. I was finally "in the door." Still, I had to push through the hard work of transitioning to white-collar work for the first time in my life.

There were steep learning curves. For example, I still was not great with computers. I took night classes at the local community college to learn computer basics.

Shortly after being hired, I was subsequently promoted to a Coordinator position, and later, to high-paying Director positions. I was moving up.

After that, I later transitioned into law school. I did this because I realized it would enhance my educational credentials, expand my knowledge base, as well as enhance my writing and legal analysis skills. I believed this would allow me to move even more easily and comfortably into the world of "Professional" men. Also, I believed that it would afford me the ability to substantively assist people as I continued on my life's journey. I absolutely wanted to help people along the way.

After graduating from law school and working as an attorney, I had the honor and privilege to save many men and women from long-term incarceration. They often faced this horrible condition which I too faced in my youth. Theirs, very often because of false allegations or unfair prosecutions. I fought numerous brutal court battles in the name of Justice, and I often won. I often held a mirror up to my opponents to show them how ugly they were behaving. I showed them how far away from justice they were. Other times I simply battered them with the law. Sometimes, very fair, honest and just opponents in the prosecutor's office fought as hard as I did to reach fair resolutions of a case. Thank you. I am pleased to have my past in the past as I continue to build the best new version of me.

CLOSING THOUGHT

A few years after release from long-term incarceration into the "Free world," I casually walked down a midtown Manhattan street. I was in New York City, headed towards one of my favorite Italian restaurants during one of my favorite times of the year, the December holiday season. I was wearing one of my favorite tailored-fitted suits, blue pinstriped. I had just parked my new, jet-black, so frequently envisioned luxury car. As a practicing criminal defense attorney, the court was traditionally slow during the holiday season. Many judges, attorneys, and other court personnel took time off during this time of year. So, I had some much-welcomed downtime. I would enjoy it.

Walking in NYC during the December holiday season, even as a young child, was always an absolute joy for me. The seemingly, million and one hanging, bright, sparkling lights, and the holiday cheer bursting in the air was still a joy.

I arrived at the beautifully styled restaurant, with the lights of NYC shining bright all around. The large Italian restaurant was filled with a festive atmosphere, as well as the fragrance of outstandingly cooked Italian food and freshly baked bread. It all smelled delicious.

I was quickly approached by the smiling restaurant staff, and I was ushered through the crowded, large establishment to my reserved table, in my favorite location within the famous restaurant—the elevated rear. I loved to sit in the rear of the restaurant, which was a bit elevated. There, I could clearly watch all the beautiful people coming and going, laughing and celebrating, enjoying life. My order was soon taken. My food promptly arrived. It looked, smelled and tasted incredible. My lovely date and I ate, drank, talked, laughed, and laughed some more. We were enjoying each other's company, enjoying life.

After a good while of conversing at the restaurant, I briefly became silent. I soon felt the eyes of my date locked intensely onto mine, she was watching me intently. After a short time, she gently grasped my hand, and while curiously staring at me, she softly asked, "Hey, what are you thinking about?"

After a brief hesitation, I looked back at her and gently grasped her hands. While looking deeply into her eyes for what seemed like a long moment, I slowly shook my head. "Nothing much," I said. "Just enjoying the evening, just enjoying life."

Made in the USA
Monee, IL
04 November 2026

67388638R10075